The Healthy H
Dog Food Cookbook

Over 60 "Beg-Worthy" Quick and Easy Dog Treat Recipes

Includes vegetarian, gluten-free and special occasion dog food recipes, BARF diet advice, general dog health and nutritional considerations

By Charlie Fox

The Healthy Homemade Dog Food Cookbook:
Over 60 "Beg-Worthy" Quick and Easy Dog Treat Recipes
Includes vegetarian, gluten-free and special occasion dog food
recipes, BARF diet advice, general dog health and nutritional
considerations

ISBN 978-1-927870-16-7

Author: Charlie Fox

Published in Canada
Printed in the USA

Foreword

This book is for dog lovers all over the world. There are many of us who truly care about our pets, their well-being and their lives entangling with ours. They are true family members and bring so much joy to all who own them.

'Dogs are our link to Paradise. They don't know evil or jealousy, or discontent. To sit with a dog on a hillside on a glorious afternoon is to be back in Eden, where doing nothing was not boring – it was peace'

— *Milan Kindera*

Acknowledgements

I would like to thank my family for inspiring the creation of this cook book. Every good dog (and naughty one too!) deserves to be spoiled and this book is dedicated to all the loyal companions out there that give so much and expect so little in return – only love, a warm cosy bed and hopefully, some tasty food!

With *SPECIAL THANKS* to these four-legged friends:-

Barkington, Ludo, Burley, Helly, Darcy and **Tinks**
and the wonderful work of The Pine Ridge Dog Sanctuary

Last, but not least – my crazy friend, **Bev,** who would adopt any furry friend who needed a good home!

Table of Contents

Introduction

A dog is a man's best friend – or so it should be. We treat them as our friends, our family and our loved ones. But are you really doing the best for your precious pet? Care of your dog includes his inside as well as his outside – exercise is wonderful, but are you providing him or her with the nutrition that he/she needs? A nutritious diet really is the only way to keep your dog in tip top health, make them happy and contented, give them the optimum energy level, a glistening coat and a smile on their faces. A well balanced diet makes a difference from top to bottom (literally!), controls obesity, tooth decay and allergenic reactions. If you start with the basics, your dog will definitely reap the benefits.

If your dog shows signs of going off their food, there is always an underlying problem – a day or so in hot weather can be a reason, but any longer than that – there's something up! We love to see our pets tucking into meals, slurping and slathering and leaving an empty bowl. Always consult with your veterinarian if you are worried – they do know best and there could be something wrong with Fido, so best to check it out.

Providing food for your dog is your responsibility and the diligence and respect that you should show them is important. They cannot do it for themselves – they are no longer wild and must rely on you to fill up the bowl with nutritious food according to their size and dietary requirements.

Please do not make the mistake of not differentiating between cooking healthy meals for your dog, or simply feeding them scraps off the plate, because you ate it. Give them real food with ingredients that are obvious and balance them as you would human food – correct levels of proteins, carbohydrates and a little fat – remember to vary the ingredients following our recipes – after all would you like to eat the same old dry food every day? Feed them twice a day (except puppies who need regular, smaller meals) – they look forward to it and the food is more digestible for them in separate lots.

Dog food manufacturers have a lot to say about why their food is best for dogs. There is nothing wrong with commercially produced dog food, but you can achieve the same and certainly better results with just a little effort yourself. By making delicious doggie dinners with love and care, pet pooch will probably get enough vitamins and minerals from what you provide for them, but remember as well that there are some great natural liquid supplements on the market that would certainly be beneficial to their health and that are completely free of any toxins. Check with your vet first the viability of your dog needing supplements.

The average lifespan of any breed of dog, taken across statistics, is around 10-11 years old, although some breeds do make it further than that. You can help your dog achieve maximum longevity by following the basic principles – diet, exercise and mental stimulation. No different to us humans really?

We hope this book helps you with all the ingredients to make your pet a happy and healthy one, and for them to give you untold pleasure in years to come.

VITAMINS AND MINERALS

These are obviously essential to your dog's health, well-being and vitality. Try working out a weekly plan to vary your pet's diet, keep up their interest so that their 'snouts' never leave the bowl when you put down one of your delicious homemade doggie dinners. A dog's digestive system in much more simple than a human system, so just a combination of the right levels of nourishment will keep them happy and satisfied.

A good combination of vitamins and minerals, plus a little fat will certainly assist in keeping Mimi's coat in tip top condition – your pet will look and feel better, and with daily grooming on top of this, you will have a prize winner. Your perfect pet is only interested in 'what's for dinner' not what's in it, but as most vitamins and minerals are all but tasteless, it really is a case of tempting their taste buds.

Meat is a rich source of protein, vitamins and minerals, but feeding meat alone to your dog just won't work. Meat also lacks other essentials such as calcium which is easily topped up by using fresh bone meal – and don't forget to add that little bit of fat, it is actually good for them. Lean meat is obviously good for them, including chicken and turkey, but you must also have the addition of 'organ meat' such as liver, kidneys, heart etc., as they contain an essential rich source of vitamins not available in the leaner variety of meats.

PROTEINS

Essential for muscle growth and healthy tissue, proteins are again found in meat, but also in fish, eggs and some dairy products, the latter three of which are easily digestible and of high usage ranking for your dogs, and tend to enter the bloodstream at a faster metabolic rate.

FATS

Fats are a must for dogs, but within moderation, as you don't want slender, athletic Rover to turn into a fat couch potato with no energy and problems such as pancreatitis and worn out joints. Fatty acids are crucial to your dogs' overall health as they regulate the immune system and are powerfully anti-inflammatory. Dogs CANNOT produce them themselves, so they must be included in the diet as they really are beneficial to most organs and also aid a healthy skin and coat. Most important fatty acids are from the Omega range, namely 3 and 6. Omega 3 is found in oily fish such as mackerel, sardines and of course the ubiquitous salmon, but can also be found in flaxseed or hempseed oil and is absorbed into the body at a reasonably fast rate, promoting healthy skin and a glistening coat. Omega 6 can be found in sunflower oil, but beware – half a tablespoon to 1 tablespoon is more than enough oil for your dogs' daily intake, depending on size.

CARBOHYDRATES

More or less 50% of your dogs' diet should include carbohydrates in some form – this can be corn, sweet potato, brown rice, oats or even soya beans and any form of whole wheat. Grains should be used more in moderation as you will see throughout the book, but they do contain essential vitamins and minerals which boost energy levels and help doggie's tummy function properly. In general, grains work on a 'slow release' basis and supply fibre to the body, assisting in healthy nerve tissue production and tip top liver, heart and brain functionality. Not all grains suit all dogs; some can be an irritant, but the only way to find this out is to try them in your recipes in small quantities. If your dog starts to react in any way, it will only be temporary, so move on to trying another grain. Probably the least irritant and mildest grain is barley, particular useful for upset tummies. Its taste and texture also seem to be extremely attractive to pooches. Likewise, Quinoa has the same settling affect on sensitive tums, and is regarded not only as a superfood for humans, but increasingly so for dogs!

NOW THE 'YES' OR 'NO' PART!

Fruit and vegetables – hmm... Lots of contentious opinions about including these in your dog's daily diet, but if owning dogs for the last 40 years, and having lots of doggie colleagues who do the same as me – yes! Do put them in their diet. Raw vegetables are not something that your dog would be interested in, to be brutally honest, so steaming or cooking them in another fashion is much more recommended, making sure they have been thoroughly washed beforehand. The only way doggie's brain would even contemplate raw vegetables would be to liquidise them to death, so they resemble baby food. Then, and only then as part of a meal, will your dog not turn his nose up.

A 'rainbow' of vegetables is recommended – different colour vegetables contain different beneficial nutrients for dogs. Leafy vegetables such as spinach, cabbage, broccoli etc are definitely beneficial, but introduce these slowly to your dog. A sudden surge of odorous cabbage into their meals will not be met with anything other than disdain, and make sure it is well mixed in and not immediately obvious!

Carrots (containing beta-carotene and Vitamin A), promote healthy eyes and provide all sorts of other essential vitamins which aid digestion and prevent *inflammation* of the stomach lining, whilst pumpkins for instance are full of anti-oxidants and also contain beta-carotene, but best of all are low in calories and really helpful as a tummy filler for dogs on a diet.

Green Beans and Peas – full of antioxidants and anti-inflammatory properties, they are also purported to be anti-carcinogenic – good source of protein and fibre.

Fruits – whilst good for dogs, they are somewhat acidic, so go easy on the portions. Water based fruits such as melon tend to be a doggie favourite, along with papaya and a small amount of mango. Apples are wonderful for dogs, follow our recipes and you will see the most popular apple recipes that your dog will just gobble up! Some small mashed up banana also does not go amiss with your furry friend, but try all of these a little at a time. Slow introduction of any foods mentioned is essential. After all, we don't all like the same foods, so why should they!

EAT, DRINK AND BE MERRY!

There is no substitute for water – just like us, dogs must have plenty of water to survive, particularly in extreme heat conditions. Water, as in humans, should be fresh at all times, even though when walking, Henry will try to find the dirtiest possible water available, normally puddles, water out of plant pots, or any other disgusting source he can find. Clean water, changed twice daily is the answer – his stomach can cope with small amounts of 'dirty' water when out walking, but do pull him or her away from it once they have had a few laps. Water keeps our doggy friends hydrated and flushes out the kidneys to aid functionality. Be wary of steams, ponds and rivers – pollution in these can harm your dog. On the other side of the coin, purified or bottled water is definitely not essential, old fashioned tap water is fine as it does contain nutrients for your dog. Stick to water – no other drinks please, even if he does like a good old cup of tea, he isn't your grannie! Like any other time, if your dog is drinking excessively and showing extreme thirst for a day or so, take them to the vet – could be, and only could be, a sign of something more sinister. Just check it out, better to be safe than sorry.

HERBS

Dogs can eat herbs, and some of the common ones are a good addition to their food mainly from a taste as much as a health point of view.

Parsley, Mint, Rosemary, Chamomile and Burdock root definitely bring out flavour in stews and casseroles, whereas thyme, celery seeds, kelp and nettles have healing properties for the digestive system and also for skin problems. Chickweed and Cleavers are also useful for skin and joint relief.

Most dogs can be seen munching through your herb garden (if you have one) and this is not such a bad thing. However, if you grow curry leaves and chillies in your garden, keep them out of your hounds' reach! It goes without saying that these could have an adverse effect on their tummies.

SEEDS

Seeds can definitely be beneficial to your dog due to their oily content and useful fats. However, they should be fed in moderation to your pet, as not all dogs can digest them. For our recipes, we only use sunflower seeds, celery seeds or sesame seeds, as these appear to be of no problems for the digestion of your dog. Take care though in providing seeds to your dog, and only use a few at a time. Moderation is the key.

100% DEFINITE NO'S IN FOOD!

NEVER feed your dog **cooked bones** – as tempting as it may be after the Sunday lunch has been cooked and all that remains is the bone with some meat on it, don't send him off into the garden to lie in the sun and munch away on his bone. They can splinter, and the result will be a mad dash to the veterinary surgery or hospital, whichever is open, to remove splintered bones from his throat. They can also lodge in the intestines, the resultant effect being a costly operation.

Dogs love bones, but feed them large raw bones. Plunge them into boiling water for a couple of minutes, as this will remove the bacteria that will have accumulated on them. If you are going to feed your dog bones, NEVER leave him unattended, be around to wrestle the bone off him is you sense problems with digestion.

If you think it's funny when your dog tries to drink out of your lunchtime or dinner tipple (as they tend to do) remove the drink immediately as **alcohol** is toxic to hounds, big or large.

Never, ever **chocolate**. Not even the tiniest bit, unless its dog chocolate. The slightest amount will, without doubt, result in fatality or an extremely ill and suffering dog.

DO NOT LEAVE YOUR **COFFEE** ON THE FLOOR IF YOU ARE RELAXING. Caffeine is dangerous for dogs to consume and can cause all sorts or seizures, strokes and even heart failure.

Fruit that has stones or pips should be 'destoned or depipped' before being fed to your dog, as much as they love their fruity treats. Digestion of these is extremely difficult for dogs and they can get lodged in the intestines.

All varieties of **onions, garlic and avocado** must be avoided as these contain sulfoxides and disulfides, all of which can cause damage to red blood cells and a very sick dog.

Grapes, raisins and mushrooms must also be avoided at all costs – the high dog-toxic content in these items can cause organ failure, toxic shock and in some cases a sad death.

Diligence is the key to keeping your dog healthy, fit and most importantly alive. You use child locks on cupboards and keep dangerous substances out of reach of tiny hands of children – you must do the same for your dog.

Nuts – another tricky one. There are too many reports regarding problems with dogs eating nuts that it is probably better not to feed any form of nut to your dog. It is a known fact that macadamia nuts are toxic, but all other nuts seem to have no real proof of goodness or otherwise.

'LEFTOVERS'

The only sensible 'leftovers' to feed your pet is what is left over from your tasty meals you have cooked for him, not what is left on your plate – i.e. no leftover curries, spicy food or anything with additives. If you have pure steamed vegetables or boiled vegetables, then great, you can use those. Best not to use any other food items that can cause an upset stomach, as tempting as it may be.

When you cook for your dog, make sure you have plenty of sealable plastic containers and bags in order to freeze any items that are not used. When you make tray bakes of treats, or if you make large quantities of doggie broth, or dinners, they will be happy sitting in the freezer for another time.

Make maximum use of your freezer when you can.

COMMERCIAL DOG FOOD VS. HOMEMADE

There is nothing wrong with manufacturer's dog food and it will not necessarily harm your pet – but there is nothing majorly right about it either. Ingredients in shop bought dog food are often of low quality or waste from other parts of the food chain. Having lived near a pet food manufacturer many years ago, you would have been horrified to see what fell off the back of the trucks transporting the food to the factory. You would not eat it, so why feed it to your beloved pet?

Commercial dog food manufacturers rely on the fact that you presume 'they know best' and use all kinds of tricks to promote their ranges. A vast amount of 'artificial' additives are included in dog food to improve the colour, texture and supposed taste. Words and phrases such as 'added vitamins' or 'premium grade' are often considered advertising tricks of the trade. There is no proof, but due to the longevity of dog food cans, there must be some kind of chemical additive to ensure that the contents do not go 'off' for months on end.

It is obviously very convenient to keep some cans of dog food in your store cupboard for emergencies or 'when you run out' of homemade food. When buying canned dog food, PLEASE READ THE LABELS! Any cheap dog foods, mean exactly that – made with cheap ingredients and stuffed full of what can only be determined as rubbish for your dogs. However, there are some wonderful ethical food manufacturers out there – so look for them.

Don't let pet food manufacturers pull the wool over your eyes – check their labels and you will be checking their integrity.

Let's go make some doggie delights!

'THE POOCH PANTRY'

Get the larder/pantry stocked with all the dry ingredients that are in most of our recipes. No point in starting then realising you haven't got what you need!

☑	Flour	All types, including wholemeal and brown rice flour, buckwheat
☑	Oils	Olive oil, vegetable oil, flaxseed oil and hempseed oil
☑	Grains/Pulses	Rice (preferably brown), quinoa, wheat germ, lentils, pearl barley, oats, ground flaxseed
☑	Cans and Jars	Salmon, tuna, sardines, mackerel all in oil, raw honey, molasses, smooth peanut butter

This will get you started. You can get small jars or packets of herbs such as parsley, ginger, turmeric, oregano, but fresh is best. Do keep them in the cupboard though as they can be used to add more flavour to doggie's dinners.

For your fridge and freezer, plenty of good quality fresh meat, preferably bought from a reputable butcher or supermarket counter. It is tempting to buy cheaper meat from a wholesaler or market, but the quality of this could be in doubt. Always ask yourself if you would eat it, and be guided by your own conscience.

Hard cheeses such as cheddar and parmesan and soft low fat cream cheese and cottage cheese are also regularly used elements in our recipes. Likewise, 0% fat plain yoghurts.

Apples, bananas, blueberries, cantaloupe melon, pumpkin, sweet potatoes, normal potatoes, carrots, cabbage, spinach and broccoli are fruits and vegetables to be kept in your vegetable locker.

This may seem a lot, but the quantities of flour and other dried goods will keep you going for some time. Vegetables and fruit of course, should be as fresh as possible at all times.

Starting with some basics, we are ready to cook!

BASIC DOG BROTH

In a lot of our dinner dishes, we use a basic broth/gravy to keep the food moist and interesting. You can make this broth and it will keep in the freezer for future use. It is up to you how much you make at a time. We have not added salt to this recipe, but if you have a fit and healthy dog, a bouillon or stock cube will give the broth a meatier flavour. In order to remove all the impurities possible, as well as a strainer, try to have some muslin on hand to strain the broth through.

- ☑ 1kg/2lb of bones (from your butcher)
- ☑ 3 carrots peeled and chopped
- ☑ 3 large potatoes, peeled and chopped
- ☑ Bunch of mixed fresh herbs, tied in a bundle
- ☑ 1 tbsp of dried kelp (if you can source it)

In a covered saucepan or stockpot, bring the bones to the boil in approximately 4 litres/7 pints of water. Once the water has boiled, turn down the heat and leave to simmer for approx 45 minutes – 1 hour.

Put the potatoes and carrots into a separate pan, bring to the boil then simmer until they are soft enough to mash down.

Sieve the bone broth using the muslin into a clean bowl, throwing away the remainders in the sieve. Combine the mashed vegetables and broth together and add the kelp.

This mix keeps in the fridge for about 5 days, or in the freezer for up to 2 months. Use small containers to freeze or use an ice cube tray.

HOMEMADE KIBBLE

Homemade kibble is infinitely superior to any store bought bags. It can be kept in the fridge in an airtight container or frozen in freezer bags for future use. We have used a high vegetable content in this recipe, but no meat. You can add minced turkey to the kibble recipe if required, but it then becomes more of a stew (another recipe for you!)

- ☑ 300 grams/9oz of brown rice, cooked to slightly overdone
- ☑ 100 grams/4oz of lentils
- ☑ 1 cup of rolled oats
- ☑ 200 grams/7oz of carrots, peeled and chopped
- ☑ 200 grams/7oz of sweet potatoes, peeled and chopped
- ☑ 2 tbsp of finely chopped parsley
- ☑ 2 cups of doggie broth (see broth recipe)
- ☑ 1 cup of powdered milk
- ☑ 2 eggs, beaten
- ☑ 1 small jar of apple puree or apple sauce (approx 100 grams/4 oz)

Cook the rice and lentils in a saucepan for approx 25 minutes. When cooked, add the carrots, sweet potatoes and apple puree to the pan. Add the oats and herbs and simmer for a further 25 minutes until most of the liquid is absorbed. The kibble should resemble a batter, thick and slightly gloopy. Add the beaten eggs and mix thoroughly.

Pour batter into a shallow baking tray and bake for about 40-45 minutes until it is dry.

Leave to cool. When cool, break into small pieces. Store in an airtight container in the fridge, and freeze however many portions you want in freezer bags.

TREATS

BREAKFASTS

AND MORE...!

OSCARS' OATIE CHEESY BISCUITS

No wheat flour in these biscuits so they suit most dogs dietary requirements!

- ☑ 225 grams/8oz fine oatmeal
- ☑ 1 tbsp of oil or fat, preferably goose fat, but dripping will do
- ☑ 1 tbsp of grated cheese
- ☑ A little warm water if required

Heat the oven to 180 C/350 F/gas mark 4. Grease a baking sheet with spray oil or a small amount of butter.

Mix the oatmeal and cheese together in a bowl, and make a well in the centre. Pour the oil or fat into the mix and mix well. If too dry, add a little hot water to make a dough.

Dust a clean work surface with a little flour and roll out the dough to approximately 1 cm/half an inch thick. Using a small cookie cutter, cut the dough into discs.

Place on the baking sheet and bake for about 15 minutes.

APPLE CINNAMON HOOPS

Most dogs love the taste of apples, so try these easy treats by drying out apple rings in the oven. The touch of cinnamon adds a sweety spice to the snack. Use a good quality apple that is not too sharp and definitely not bruised.

- ☑ 3 Large Apples
- ☑ Several light 'shakes' of cinnamon

Heat the oven to 160 C/320 F/gas mark 3.

Peel and core the apples, making sure the pips are all removed. Slice into rings. Sprinkle each slice with cinnamon, like a dusting.

Place on a baking tray into the oven and bake for about 4 hours. The texture of the apples should be dry and a bit chewy, and not crisped up. They will keep in an airtight container for about 3 weeks, but knowing dogs, they won't last that long!

LUSCIOUS LIVER TRAY BAKE

Delicious tray bake with tasty and nutritional chicken livers. Cut into pieces, you can freeze them for up to a month or they will stay fine in the fridge for 5 days. The size you cut them is up to you. This make a large tray bake.

- ☑ 2 cups of wholemeal flour
- ☑ 1 cup of plain flour
- ☑ 3 eggs, beaten
- ☑ Half a cup of oatmeal
- ☑ 500 grams/ 1lb 2 oz of chicken livers.
- ☑ A little water if required
- ☑ 1 tbsp of oil

Preheat oven to 160 C/320 F.

Dice the liver into smallish pieces and gently fry on a low heat with 1 tbsp of oil. Place all the other ingredients into a bowl, and mix well. Tip in the liver when it is cooked, and mix again. Should form a cake like consistency. Pour or spoon into a low sided baking tray and place in the oven for about 20 minutes.

Remove and cool, as it will harden slightly when cooling. Cut into mouthful size pieces, let doggie taste them, then refrigerate or freeze the rest in freezer bags.

POOCHES PORRIDGE

Oats are a great ingredient for dogs, very high in protein and easy on their digestive systems. If your dogs have a 'workout', replace their energy with oats! So that the oats have a chance to cool down, try to remember to cook them the night before and leave in the fridge.

- ☑ 100 grams/4ozs of oats
- ☑ 1 grated apple
- ☑ Handful of blueberries
- ☑ 1 tbsp of wheat germ or flaxseed
- ☑ Half a teaspoon of raw honey

Simmer the oats in 600ml/1 pint of water for about 5-6 minutes. Leave to cool for an hour or so, or overnight.

Mix the grated apple and blueberries in with the oats, top with wheat germ or flaxseed, whichever suits.

DELICIOUS DOGGY BISCUITS

Dogs seems to love these, not sure why, but they do! Try using these with our doggie dip, and you won't see a scrap left! Buy some dog bone shaped cutters or other shape – there are lots on the market.

- ☑ 2 and half cups of whole wheat flour
- ☑ 1 teaspoon of brown sugar
- ☑ Half cup of powdered milk
- ☑ 6 tablespoons of butter
- ☑ 1 egg, beaten
- ☑ Half teaspoon of dried mixed herbs
- ☑ Half cup of ice water

Mix the flour, milk and sugar together and add the butter. Combine together until the mixture looks smooth but textured. Mix in the beaten egg.

Slowly add the water until the mixture comes together in a ball. On a lightly floured surface, press down the dough to about half an inch/1.2 cms thick. Using your cookie cutters, make as many as you can, using up any scraps of dough together to finish off any remains.

Heat the oven to 175 C/350 F. Place the dog biscuits on to an lightly oiled tray and place in the oven for 25 minutes. Leave to cool on a wire rack.

DAMN DELICIOUS DIP!

This dip is finger licking (or paw licking) good with our biscuits. You can either just dip the biscuits into the mix or, dip them in totally and leave in the fridge. The coating will harden around the biscuits, almost like icing but not so sweet!

- ☑ 3 tbsp of smooth peanut butter
- ☑ 2 tbsp of raw honey
- ☑ 1 very ripe banana, mashed
- ☑ 2 cups of low fat vanilla yoghurt
- ☑ 1 tbsp whole wheat flour

Mix the yoghurt and flour together to form a smooth paste. In a separate bowl, mix the banana, honey and peanut butter or use a blender until smooth.

Add the fruit mix to the yogurt mix and blend together thoroughly. Refrigerate to keep cold. (At this stage, coat the biscuits if you want and lay on a plate or tray).

CHICKEN LIVER STRIPPERS

These are very easy to make and dogs just gobble them up. If you have any bits of left over liver when you are making other recipes, or you just feel like giving a tasty chewy treat to your dog, these are ideal. These are great as a training treat, or just any treat for your pet.

☑ Quantity of chicken livers, cut into strips

Heat the oven to 180 C/360 F. Place the strips of chicken livers on to a lightly oiled baking tray and place in the oven.

Cook for at least 30 minutes, until the strips are drying out and looking a little 'leathery'.

Remove from the oven and continue to dry out at room temperature. The strips will not look exactly pretty, but they go down very well with your doggie!

Keep in a freezer bag in the fridge. They will not last long enough for you to bother freezing them, but use sparingly!

PORK AND APPLE POPS

Delicious treats, try to get the leanest possible pork mince or sausage meat. We have used sticks to set the pops on before cooking, but make sure you remove the stick before feeding to your dog.

- ☑ 500 grams/ 1lb 2oz minced pork/sausage meat
- ☑ 1 peeled and grated apple
- ☑ Half teaspoon of mixed spice (such as pumpkin pie spice, or use nutmeg or cinnamon)
- ☑ Flour for dusting
- ☑ Cocktail sticks

Heat the oven to 160 C/320 F. Lightly oil a flat baking tray.

In a mixing bowl, put the sausage meat, grated apple and mixed spice. Mix together thoroughly. If the mixture is too wet, add a little wholemeal flour to bind together.

Form the mixture into balls, about 3.5cm/1 and a half inches circumference. Thread the cocktail stick through until about half way so the ball sits on top of the stick.

Place on the tray and bake in the oven for 25 minutes. Remove and leave to cool. Remove the stick before feeding.

FIDO'S FRUITY SALAD

Cottage cheese and mixed fruit with lightly toasted wheat germ, or a probiotic supplement makes this a doggy delight. Easy on the tummy which adds digestion.

- ☑ 225 gram/8 oz tub of low fat cottage cheese
- ☑ Handful of blueberries
- ☑ Half an ogen melon, chopped into small pieces (without skin!)
- ☑ 2 tablespoons of toasted wheat germ or probiotic supplement

Prepare your melon, making sure that all seeds have been removed.

In a mixing bowl, pour the cottage cheese and add the melon and blueberries. Mix well together. Add half the wheat germ/probiotic and mix again.

Top the dish with the remaining wheat germ/probiotic – doggy will love the smell!

CHAMPAGNE CHARLIE'S BREAKFAST
(without the champagne!)

A take on a champagne breakfast, tasty salmon is mixed with scrambled eggs for a true melting moment in the mouth!

- ☑ 3 eggs, beaten
- ☑ 1 small can of salmon (no need to remove the bones)
- ☑ 1 tablespoon of fresh chopped parsley
- ☑ Small handful of fresh spinach
- ☑ 25 grams / 1 oz of butter

Open the can of salmon, drain off most of the liquid and put into a bowl.

Heat a frying pan with the butter until it has melted, then pour in the beaten eggs.

Once the eggs begin to cook but are still liquid, put in the spinach and stir to mix.

Place the salmon and parsley into the egg mixture and continue to cook, stirring to avoid sticking.

Once the eggs are scrambled and everything is combined together, remove from the pan and leave to cool before serving.

CORNY CARROT MUFFINS

These yummy muffins will make your dog smile (tempting to eat them yourself!)

- ☑ 4 cups of whole wheat flour
- ☑ 1 tbsp of baking powder
- ☑ 3 cups of water
- ☑ 1 egg
- ☑ 2 tbsp of raw honey
- ☑ 1 tbsp cinnamon
- ☑ 1 tbsp nutmeg
- ☑ 2 medium sized carrots, grated.
- ☑ Half tablespoon of brown sugar
- ☑ 1 large banana (very ripe or overripe) or jar of banana baby food

Heat the oven to 175C/350F.

Mix all the 'wet' ingredients together in a bowl making sure that everything is combined. Place to one side.

In a separate bowl, combine all the 'dry' ingredients, then mix the wet mixture into the dry, ensuring that everything is bound together.

Lightly grease or oil a 12 portion muffin tin (very lightly please!) Fill each hole up to about three-quarters full.

Bake in the oven for 50 minutes.

SPANIEL SPANISH OMELETTE – YARIBA!!

A twist on a traditional Spanish omelette, pooch will be pampered with this dish.

- ☑ 3 eggs, beaten
- ☑ 1 large cooked potato, in small chunks
- ☑ 1 large cooked sweet potato, in small chunks
- ☑ Small handful of cooked green beans
- ☑ 1 tbsp of chopped parsley
- ☑ 1 tbsp of olive oil or a strong spray of oil to prevent sticking

Heat your grill, to medium heat.

Heat a frying pan over a low heat. When the oil is warmed through, pour in your eggs and make the omelette as you would normally do. Just as the omelette is beginning to set, scatter the vegetables over the omelette to warm through.

For the final 30 seconds or so, place the pan under the grill and the omelette will 'soufflé' up a little. Remove from the grill, tip on to a plate and fold.

When the omelette has cooled, slice into mouth-sized strips – OLE!!

CHICKEN STRIPPERS

If you are having a chicken meal yourself, using chicken breasts, make sure you buy an extra one! Lean skinless and boneless chicken breast is used here in this slightly 'indulgent' treat.

- ☑ 1 lean, skinless, boneless chicken breast, cut into strips
- ☑ 1 teaspoon of sesame seeds
- ☑ Half a very finely chopped parsnip
- ☑ A little oil

Heat the oven to 170 C/340 F.

In a bowl place a little oil and mix in the chicken strips, sesame seeds and finely chopped parsnip. (The parsnip should be in very tiny cube shaped pieces).

Lightly grease a baking tray and place the strippers on to the tray – any bits left in the bowl, lightly scatter over the top of the strips.

Place in the oven and cook for about 15 minutes until firm but not dried out.

Leave to cool before serving. These can be served as part of a main meal or as a treat. Any small pieces of parsnip can be scraped off the tray and served on top of the strippers.

'ON THE GO' CHEESY BREAKFAST BARS

Take these in the car with you as a substitute for breakfast if you are in a hurry. They are by no means enough for a full breakfast if you have a large dog, but they can supply a filling stop gap until you have time to feed.

- ☑ 200 grams/7 oz of rolled oats
- ☑ 2 tbsp raw honey
- ☑ 120 grams/3oz of grated cheddar cheese
- ☑ 2 and a half tablespoons of sunflower oil (olive oil is a little heavy for this recipe)
- ☑ 1 teaspoon of chopped fresh parsley, rosemary or oregano
- ☑ 1 egg, beaten

Lightly grease a baking tin.

Heat your oven to 180 C/250 F.

Place all the ingredients into a pan and stir over a low heat for a few minutes until combined and softened.

Pour into the baking tray and press down with the back of a spoon or spatula.

Bake for approximately 20 minutes – they should be golden brown.

Remove from the oven and leave to cool. Cut into bar sized slices, or smaller if you prefer. The bars/squares will be fine in an airtight container in the fridge for about two weeks, but they won't last that long!

TASTY TUNA TEMPTATIONS

We have never met a dog yet that doesn't like fish! Is it the smell or the texture? Who knows!

- ☑ 200 gram/8oz tin of tuna in oil, definitely not brine
- ☑ 100 gram/4oz flour
- ☑ 1 egg, beaten

Heat your oven to 350C/180 F. Lightly oil or grease a low sided baking tray.

Drain off most of the oil from the tuna and mash into a bowl. Add the beaten egg and stir thoroughly to mix in.

Add the flour, stirring until the mixture forms a dough like consistency.

Roll the dough into small balls and place on the baking tray. Bake in the oven for 20 minutes – they should be golden brown.

Store for up to 2 weeks in the fridge in an airtight container. You can substitute tuna for salmon, mackerel or sardines, in fact any fish that you want.

VERY VEGGIE BONES

A vegetarian bone mix for your dog, if for any reason they cannot or will not eat meat. Still tasty though for the less discerning dog!

- ☑ 3 cups of all-purpose flour
- ☑ Half a cup of grated carrots
- ☑ 2 tablespoons of bran
- ☑ 2 teaspoons of baking powder
- ☑ Half a cup of grated cheese (cheddar or even mozzarella)
- ☑ 2 cups of finely chopped or minced parsley
- ☑ Half a cup of finely chopped rosemary
- ☑ Half a cup of water
- ☑ 2 tablespoons of olive oil

Heat oven to 180 C/350 F. Lightly grease a baking sheet.

Stir together the herbs, carrots, oil and cheese in one bowl. In another bowl, mix together the dry ingredients and then tip into the wet. Mix thoroughly. Add the water gradually to form a moist, but not wet dough. If you need more water, do so a little at a time.

Knead the dough for 1 minute or so, then roll out to approx half an inch thick/1.2 cm.

Using a bone shaped cutter, cut out the bones and place on the baking sheet. If you have any bits and pieces left, re-roll and cut out more shapes.

Bake for 25 minutes until the bones are golden brown and crisp. Leave for a little longer if required, but remember they do harden more when removed from the oven.

Store in an airtight container, they will keep for a few weeks.

VICTOR'S VEGGIE CRISPS

Lovely vegetarian potato and vegetable chips, very easy and a good way of using up any root vegetables you may have such as potatoes, sweet potatoes, parsnip, etc. Again, you would probably enjoy these yourself with a slight sprinkling of sea salt! Experiment as well with very thin slices of fresh beetroot, extremely good for dogs, especially those with any liver complaints.

- ☑ Selection of root vegetables, as above, thinly sliced in rings or thin pieces
- ☑ A sprinkling of olive oil

Heat the oven to 170 C/350 F.

Put all the sliced vegetables into a bowl, and pour over a little olive oil to coat them. Mix the vegetables around in the oil so that they are all covered.

Spread the slices out evenly and not overlapping on to a baking tray. Bake in the oven for about 50 minutes, making sure they do not burn. Remove from the oven and leave to cool. They should be slightly crisp but not hard. Store in an airtight container, out of the fridge.

Try using them with our doggie dip!

MINTY MEAT BALLS

These treats not only taste delicious, they smell great when you are cooking them!

Also helps doggie's breath smell a bit sweeter with the addition of fresh chopped mint. Experiment using chicken or turkey mince, even beef mince with a different herb such as parsley. You could also try substituting the rice flour with a wholemeal stuffing mix which generally already contain herbs.

- ☑ 300 grams/12 oz of lean minced lamb
- ☑ 1 egg
- ☑ 50 grams/2oz brown rice flour
- ☑ 1 tsp of chopped fresh mint

Heat the oven to 180 C/360 F.

If you have a food processor you can use this, but as we like to be messy (!) doing it by hand is much more satisfying!

Whichever way, mix all the ingredients together to form a 'dough like' consistency, if you are using a food processor. If not, simply mix all the ingredients together with a mixing spoon to form a dough with a lot more texture.

Roll into small balls, the size is up to you. Place on a lightly oiled baking tray and chill for about 30 minutes.

Remove from the fridge and cook in the oven for about 40 minutes, they should have a crunchy exterior but still be slightly soft in the middle. Make sure you put the meatballs on kitchen paper to drain off any fat.

PERFECT PUMPKIN ROSETTES

These small bite sized treats are great for training and also for dogs on a vegetarian diet.

- ☑ 450 grams/16 oz of pumpkin (you can use canned pumpkin, but fresh is best)
- ☑ Half cup of rice cereal
- ☑ Quarter cup of powdered milk
- ☑ Half cup of oatmeal
- ☑ A little water if required

Heat oven to 150 C/300 F. Lightly grease a flat baking tray.

Mix all the ingredients until smooth and well combined. Time to get out your piping bag with nozzle!

Fill the bag with the mixture, and pipe out small rosette shapes, about 2.4 cm/ 1 inch in diameter. You can make them bigger if you want.

Bake the rosettes in the oven for approx. 20 minutes, slightly longer if you make the rosettes bigger.

Cool completely, store in an airtight container until needed.

DELICIOUS

DOGGIE

DINNERS

ROVER'S CHICKEN RISOTTO

A slight 'Caribbean' influence to this one, rice and peas with the addition of pumpkin and a little nutmeg. Lip-licking delicious!

- ☑ 2 large skinless and boneless chicken breasts
- ☑ 350 grams/6oz green beans, cut into pieces
- ☑ 225 grams/4oz frozen peas
- ☑ 225 grams/4oz pumpkin
- ☑ 225 grams/4oz rice
- ☑ 1 teaspoon of nutmeg
- ☑ Half teaspoon of turmeric
- ☑ 1 cup of low-salt chicken gravy

Poach the chicken breasts in water in the oven making sure that the water covers the breasts. Poach for 25-30 minutes, remove from the oven to cool.

While the chicken is cooking, cook the rice as per packet instructions with the turmeric, about 10- 15 minutes until tender. Drain and rinse.

Cook the fresh green beans in water until tender. Cook the pumpkin, in small pieces in water until tender. When the beans are just becoming tender, put the peas in the same pot to defrost and warm through.

When vegetables are all cooked, drain and set aside. In a large bowl, mix the rice and vegetables together, add the chicken, diced into small mouth sized pieces, and follow this with the nutmeg. Mix well.

Heat the gravy until warm, then pour over the meat and vegetable dish and mix thoroughly. Leave to cool slightly and serve.

The dish will keep in the fridge for up to 4 days.

YANKEE NOODLE DANDY

Dogs normally love pasta and noodles, but they should not be used as part of their regular daily diet, more as a treat. With this dish, only about a quarter of the dish is made up of the noodles, the rest is comprised of beef and vegetables.

- ☑ 110 grams/2oz of soba noodles (buckwheat)
- ☑ 225 grams/4oz lean beef mince
- ☑ Handful of shredded curly kale or cabbage
- ☑ 110 grams/2oz of grated carrot
- ☑ 110 grams/2 oz of cooked chopped green beans
- ☑ A little olive oil
- ☑ Half tablespoon of ground flax seed

Dry fry the beef with a little olive oil, making sure you break up the clumps. Add a little water and continue to stir until the meat is cooked. Pour off the excess fat.

In a separate pot, cook the kale or cabbage with a little water. Add the green beans and continue to cook until tender. Stir in the grated carrot and flax seed. Set aside.

Plunge the noodles into hot water and leave to soak for a couple of minutes. Drain and cut into small pieces, and mix in with the beef and vegetables. Serve when cool.

HUNGRY HOUND HASH

A very wholesome dish for your dog with the addition of oils for aiding joint movement and coat condition.

- ☑ 120 grams/4oz brown rice
- ☑ 50 grams/2oz porridge oats
- ☑ 300 grams/12oz lean beef mince
- ☑ A couple of handfuls of spinach
- ☑ 2 small apples, peeled, cored and grated
- ☑ 1 tablespoon of chopped fresh herbs
- ☑ 25 grams/1oz ground flaxseed
- ☑ Half tablespoon of salmon oil

Cook the rice in approximately 600ml/1 pint of water, for about 20 minutes, then stir in the porridge oats and leave for about 5 minutes.

Brown the beef mince in a frying pan until cooked through, making sure you break down any clumps. Cook the spinach in a little water until just soft, drain off any excess water.

Put the rice and oats, mince, greens and grated apple into a big bowl and mix thoroughly. Add the flaxseed, herbs and salmon oil and mix again.

Serve when cool. We do not recommend freezing this dish, so if there is any left, store in the fridge for up to 4 days.

COMFORTING KEDGEREE

Plain fish and rice is exceptionally good at all times for your dog, but particularly if they have had a bad tummy for any reason. Vets always recommend something soothing for the stomach such as boiled or poached fish, or chicken. Not an advocate of boiling where possible, we tend to poach the fish in water or a little milk.

- ☑ 225 grams/4 oz of white fish fillets, such as coley, cod, haddock
- ☑ 200 grams/3 oz of brown rice
- ☑ 1 carrot, peeled and finely chopped
- ☑ Handful of peas
- ☑ 1 tablespoon of salmon oil
- ☑ 2 tablespoons of low fat plain yoghurt
- ☑ 1 egg, hard boiled

Heat the oven to 160 C/320 F.

Wrap the fish fillets in aluminium foil with a little water, to form a packet. Put on a tray into the oven and cook for 15 minutes. Unwrap the package to make sure the fish is cooked and moist.

In the meantime, cook the rice as per packet instructions, rinse and drain. Cook the frozen peas until tender.

Flake the fish into the rice mixture, add the parsley, salmon oil and peas. Mix the yoghurt into the mixture.

Finely chop the hard-boiled egg and scatter over the top of the dish. Ready to serve when cool enough.

TEMPTING TUNA BAKE

You can also make this dish with salmon; both fish are vitamin and nutrient rich and provide health benefits to your dog.

- ☑ 200 gram/7oz tin of tuna in oil or spring water (not brine)
- ☑ 200 gram/7oz carrots
- ☑ 2 apples, peeled, cored and grated
- ☑ 250 grams/9 oz sweet potatoes, peeled and chopped
- ☑ 100 grams/4oz of oats
- ☑ 100grams/4oz of plain natural low fat yoghurt
- ☑ 1 egg, beaten
- ☑ 1 tablespoon of probiotic supplement or ground flaxseed

Preheat oven to 180 C/350 F.

Cook the sweet potatoes in water until soft, drain and mash.

Put the oats in a pan and cook for 10 minutes, or as per packet instructions.

Put the tuna into a large bowl, mash and then add the potatoes and the oats.

Mix thoroughly. Stir in the apples, grated carrot, yoghurt and egg. Mix again very thoroughly

Pour or spoon the mixture into a baking dish, smooth down a little and sprinkle with the probiotic or flaxseed.

Allow to cool before serving. Will stay fresh in the fridge for up to 4 days.

IRISH LAMB HOTPOT

Based on a traditional Irish dish, this lamb hotpot is super for dogs, they will be licking the bowl all around the kitchen!

- ☑ 450 grams/ 1 lb of lean lamb, diced for casseroling or stewing
- ☑ 4 large potatoes, peeled and thinly sliced
- ☑ 3 carrots, peeled and sliced diagonally, quite thinly
- ☑ 1 cupful of tinned cooked lentils, washed to remove any salt
- ☑ I cupful of pearl barley, cooked as per packet instructions
- ☑ 2 cups of doggie broth
- ☑ 1 low salt lamb stock cube
- ☑ 1 teaspoon of fresh chopped rosemary

Put the lamb in a stockpot and cover with water. Bring to the boil and leave to simmer for about 1hr and 30 minutes, until the lamb is so tender that it shreds. Top up the water during cooking if beginning to run down.

While the lamb is cooking, prepare the pearl barley as per packet instructions. Drain and set aside. Put your carrots and potatoes into a pan of water and cook until tender. It does not matter if they break up a little, this is what hotpot looks like!

When the lamb is tender, drain through a sieve to remove the fatty liquid. Add the lamb to the cooked vegetables, pearl barley and lentils.

Heat the doggie stock with the lamb stock cube and rosemary, until dissolved, stirring to remove any lumps, then add the stock to the lamb mixture. Serve when cool. If you want, you can add a little chopped fresh mint to the dish as well.

Freeze any remaining dish for up to 1 month, or store in the fridge for 4 to 5 days.

SALMON AND TUNA MEATLOAF

Another doggie delight – delicious salmon and tuna baked in a loaf tin in the oven. Use a 900 gram/1lb loaf tin non-stick loaf tin.

- ☑ 225 grams/8oz canned salmon
- ☑ 225 grams/8oz canned tuna (in oil or spring water, definitely not brine)
- ☑ 1 egg, beaten
- ☑ 1 carrot, finely diced
- ☑ 1 stick of celery, finely diced
- ☑ 1 teaspoon of fresh chopped parsley
- ☑ 1 and half tablespoons of low fat cottage cheese
- ☑ 1 cup of wholemeal breadcrumbs

Heat your oven to 180 C/350 F.

Mix all of the ingredients together, making sure the tuna and salmon is mashed and combined with everything else. If the mixture is too wet, add some more breadcrumbs, if a little dry, add a small amount of water.

Lightly grease the loaf tin, then pour in the mixture and press down to make it compact.

Bake in the oven for 40-45 minutes until firm to the touch. Leave to cool and then slice into pieces.

The loaf can be stored in the fridge for a couple of days, or up to 2 weeks in the freezer.

MIGHTY MEATY MUTT LOAF

When this is cooking in the oven, the whole family presume it's for them! The aroma is delicious and you dog will be waiting patiently for it to come out of the oven!

- ☑ 450 grams/1lb of minced beef (try to get no more than 10% fat)
- ☑ 200 grams/7oz chicken livers
- ☑ 150 grams/5oz carrots, peeled and grated
- ☑ 400 grams/14oz potatoes, peeled and grated (you can use half sweet potatoes)
- ☑ 2 eggs, beaten
- ☑ 1 tablespoon of chopped fresh rosemary
- ☑ 50 grams/ 2oz oats

Preheat the oven to 180 C/350 F. Simmer the chicken livers in water for a few minutes, drain and chop into small pieces.

Mix the minced beef, grated potato and carrot together, then add the livers into a bowl.

Add the beaten eggs, oats and herbs into the meat mixture, mixing with a spoon or with your hands (clean please!)

Pour the mixture into a greased loaf tin, and press gently down, smoothing the top as well.

Bake for 1 hour and 15 minutes – test to make sure the loaf is firm. Remove from the oven and when cooled enough to handle, pour off any excess fat. When totally cool, remove the loaf from the tin and slice.

Can be stored in the freezer for up to 2 months, and in the fridge for 5 days or so.

FISHCAKE FEAST

These are great to make in advance and store in the freezer. Use any white fish, whatever is the cheapest option that you can locally source (coley, cod, haddock). The best idea is when you are thinking about fish for yourselves, buy some extra and turn into fishcakes for your hound. You can make your own fish pie at the same time!

- ☑ 450 grams/1lb of white fish, fillets or deboned
- ☑ 3 large potatoes, peeled, diced and cooked
- ☑ 1 tablespoon of chopped parsley
- ☑ Half a cup of peas
- ☑ Handful of spinach leaves
- ☑ 1 cup of wholemeal breadcrumbs
- ☑ Small quantity of milk to cover the fish

Poach the fish in a pan on the top of the oven in some milk (use enough milk to cover the fish in the pan) For the last minute or so, put the spinach in the pan to soften. Turn off the fish and leave.

Mash the potatoes using a little of the poaching fluid. Mix in the fish by flaking it into the bowl. Add the chopped parsley, and peas. Drain off the spinach from the pan and mix in with the rest of the ingredients. Stir thoroughly to make sure the mixture is evenly distributed.

Put the breadcrumbs on a clean surface or board. Shape the mixture into fishcakes (whatever size you want) and then roll in the breadcrumbs.

Place in a preheated oven 170 C/350 F, and bake for about ten minutes to crisp up the outsides. Leave to cool and then break into pieces to serve.

Can be frozen for up to 2 weeks.

SARDINE SURPRISE

Lovely and really quick sardine dish, full of nutrients for your dog. Always use sardines in oil, never in tomato sauce. This can be made in the microwave.

- ☑ 2 tins of sardines in oil
- ☑ Half a cup of rolled oats
- ☑ Half a courgette/zucchini, grated
- ☑ Half a carrot, grated

Mix all the ingredients together. For a smooth 'cake', blend them in a processor. If you want texture, just mix them all together yourself in a bowl.

The mixture should be 'cake' consistency or pudding consistency. Add a little flour if necessary. It is not the most attractive mix, but the taste certainly is for doggie!

Microwave the mix for approx 5 minutes and leave to cool. Serve when cool.

Not recommended for freezing, but can be left in the fridge for a couple of days.

CHICKEN AND BARLEY STEW

Quite a comforting dish and full of goodness. The vegetable content contains a lot of beta-carotene, which also aids a wonderful glossy and healthy coat for your dog.

- ☑ 1 whole chicken
- ☑ 300 grams/10 oz of carrots, peeled and chopped
- ☑ 3 apples, peeled, de-cored, de-seeded and chopped
- ☑ 500 grams/ 1lb 2oz of sweet potatoes, chopped
- ☑ 120 grams/ 4oz pearl barley, washed and cooked, then drained (30 minutes)
- ☑ 1 teaspoon of ground flaxseed
- ☑ Bouquet garni – parsley, rosemary tied in a bunch

Take a very large pan or stock pot, and place the whole chicken into the pot and cover with water. Put the bouquet garni into the pot. Bring to the boil, turn down to simmer and place a lid on the pan. Simmer for about 1 hour and 15 minutes. When cool enough to handle, drain off the stock through a sieve, leaving the chicken to one side. The stock should be quite clear of any excess fat.

Prepare all the vegetables as instructed. Place into the stock, and cook until tender.

Pull all the chicken meat off the skin, discarding any skin or grizzly bits.

Mix everything together, just like a stew you would eat yourself – in fact you can!

Serve in a wonderful doggie bowl, and sprinkle with the flaxseed on top. Guaranteed to make your dog smile and warm from the inside to out!

Keep in the fridge for up to 5 days, or freeze for up to 2 months.

TASTY TURKEY CROQUETTES

These can be made with turkey or chicken or minced beef, whichever you have. Dogs will love them whatever the ingredients are! You can also use good quality sausage meat.

- ☑ 450 grams/1 lb of turkey mince (or beef, chicken, lamb)
- ☑ 1 large sweet potato, peeled and chopped into small pieces
- ☑ 1 large potato, peeled and chopped into small pieces
- ☑ Teaspoon of chopped parsley or mint
- ☑ 1 teaspoon of olive oil

Dry fry the turkey mince in a frying pan. If needs be, add a little olive oil.

Cook and mash the potatoes together, mix in the herbs.

Mix together the turkey and the potato mix, making sure they are evenly combined. Add a little olive oil and mix again.

Lightly flour a board or your work surface. Take a small handful of the mix, roll into a ball and then into 'sausage shapes'.

Place on a greased baking sheet and bake in the oven for 25 minutes. Remove and allow to cool.

Can be frozen for up to one month, or served as soon as cool. Try serving with some ready cooked vegetables and a little doggie broth.

CANINE COTTAGE PIE

A twist on English Shepherd's pie, yummy scrummy doggie dish with beef mince and sweet potatoes – a wholesome dish that your pampered pooch will woof up!

- ☑ 450 grams/1lb of lean minced beef
- ☑ 2 large sweet potatoes
- ☑ 2 sticks of celery, chopped
- ☑ Handful of peas
- ☑ 1 carrot, diced
- ☑ 1 cup of doggie broth

Whilst pan frying beef is fine, vary cooking minced beef by bringing to the boil in water, and then simmering until cooked. Rinse off the beef through a sieve, to remove any excess fat or scum. Leave to one side.

In a clean pan, put in the diced celery and carrot in enough water to cover them, and cook until slightly tender. Drain off the water and mix in the vegetables with the meat.

Cook your sweet potatoes as normal until tender, and then drain off the liquid.

Mix in a little doggie broth with the mince and vegetables, then top the meat mix with the sweet potatoes.

Can be left in the fridge for up to 5 days, or frozen in bags or containers for up to 2 months.

CHAMPIONS CHICKEN RISOTTO

A super recipe. Have a look in your vegetable store and see what vegetables you have ready to use up, such as green beans, broccoli, carrots, parsnip etc. Any of these vegetables will do to make up this lovely risotto medley. We use normal brown rice, with a touch of turmeric.

- ☑ 1 cup of brown rice
- ☑ 1 large chicken breast, poached in water
- ☑ 1 large carrot, peeled and chopped
- ☑ 50 grams/2 oz green beans, chopped
- ☑ 1 head of broccoli, trimmed but with some stalk
- ☑ Half teaspoon of turmeric
- ☑ Half teaspoon of mixed dried herbs
- ☑ 1 cup of doggie broth

Cook brown rice with the turmeric according to packet instructions, about 25 minutes until tender. Drain, wash off and set aside.

Heat the oven to 170 C/ 340 F. Poach a large chicken breast in a dish in the oven, making sure the breast is covered with the water. Takes approx 25-30 minutes to cook through. Remove and set aside, after draining off the poaching liquid.

Cook the carrots and green beans in water until half tender, then add the broccoli until all vegetables are soft.

Chop the chicken breast into small slices, mix with the rice and vegetables and add one cup of doggie broth and the herbs. Bring up to the boil again, stir and simmer for a few minutes then remove from the heat.

Stir again before serving.

Can be kept in the fridge for up to 5 days. Freeze for 2 weeks.

PARTY TIME – HARIBA!!

Based on a paella, and introducing prawns/shrimp into your dog's diet, this is another rice based dish with plenty of nutrients. Make up a large batch and invite his or her friends round for a party! If you are not going to feed more than one dog, use the recipe below, as we do not recommend freezing as the prawns used have been frozen originally and should not be re-frozen. We have used a little chopped tomatoes in this dish as they are skinless and cause no harm in small quantities.

- ☑ 1 tin of mackerel in oil
- ☑ 1 whole chicken breast
- ☑ 6 large shrimp (prawns) defrosted and cut in half or thirds (depending on size)
- ☑ 1 cup of brown rice
- ☑ 1 cup of doggie broth
- ☑ 1 can of French beans, chopped
- ☑ 110 grams/ 2oz of chopped tinned tomatoes (no salt variety)

Poach the chicken breast in the oven for approx. 25-30 minutes until cooked through. Remove from the oven and cool. Cut into mouth sized slices.

Cook the rice as per packed instructions, about 25-30 minutes until tender. Drain and set aside.

In a clean bowl, mix the chicken with the mackerel, shredded, and the prawns. Slice and chop the French beans and add to the bowl. Mix in the chopped tomatoes, a little at a time without much juice. Mix the rice through the mix and add a cup of the doggie broth and leave to soak for a little while.

OLE !! Just multiply this mix according to how many dogs you are feeding!

COWBOY CHOWDOWN

A 'take' on pork and beans, this is a healthy meal for your dog, using a limited amount of 'legumes' (beans) to add some soluble, digestible protein and to aid heart and circulation.

- ☑ 250 grams/half pound of minced pork
- ☑ 1 carrot, finely diced
- ☑ 1 courgette/zucchini finely diced
- ☑ 110 grams/4 oz of pinto beans/borlotti/flageolet beans, from a tin, but rinsed to remove any salt
- ☑ Handful of finely shredded cabbage
- ☑ 1 cup of low salt chicken gravy
- ☑ Olive oil

Lightly pan fry the pork mince in the pan using a small amount of olive oil. Make sure you break up the pork so that it cooks evenly throughout.

Add the carrot and cabbage, pour in the gravy. Stir regularly, reducing the heat and simmer for 5 minutes. Add the grated zucchini/courgette and continue to simmer for a further 5 minutes. Just before serving, add the beans to heat through.

Serve slightly warm or room temperature.

Leave in the fridge for 4 days, or freeze until needed.

PARTY TIME!

MIGHTY MEUSLI STYLE MOUTHFULS

These really are a 'sweet' tasting treat and full of goodness and essential vitamins such as B and C. The blackstrap molasses also add a good source of iron.

- ☑ 200 grams/7 oz of oats
- ☑ 3 tbsp of sunflower oil
- ☑ 1 tbsp blackstrap molasses
- ☑ 1 tbsp of ground rosehips (try to get these, they are available in health food shops and add a wonderful dimension to the treat recipe)
- ☑ 100 grams/4 oz of apple baby food
- ☑ 50 grams/2 oz of ground sunflower seeds

Preheat the oven to 180 C/350 F. Lightly oil or grease a oil a baking tin.

In a bowl, mix the apple baby food, oil, molasses and rosehips together.

Pour the ground sunflower seeds and oats into a saucepan and stir to combine.

Mix the apple mix and oats mix together in the saucepan, stirring continuously until the mixture is all melted together, should be a nice thick gooey mess!

Pour the mix into the baking tray and flatten down with the back of a spoon. Place the tray in the oven and bake for approximately 20 minutes – the mixture should be a lovely golden brown.

Remove from the oven and leave to cool. Cut into squares or bars and store in the fridge for up to a week in an airtight container.

PEANUT BUTTER SQUIRRELS

Have fun cutting these into shapes – we have cut ours into squirrels! You can use any shaped cutter that you want, it's all about enjoying and pampering your dog.

Dogs love peanut butter and the biscuits smell delicious when cooking in the oven.

☑ 2 cups of spelt flour
☑ 2 cups of rice flour
☑ 6 heaped tablespoons of peanut butter
☑ 1 large egg
☑ 2 tablespoons of raw honey

Heat the oven to 180 C/350 F.

In a large bowl, mix all of the ingredients together, making sure they are completely combined and looking like a cookie dough mix. If the dough is a little dry, add a touch of water, if a little wet, add a touch more flour.

Turn out on to a very lightly floured work surface and knead for just a couple of minutes to make sure everything is mixed together. Roll out to about 1cm/slightly less than half an inch thick. Cut out your squirrels (or whatever animal cookie cutter you may have!)

Bake in the oven for 15-20 minutes. Leave to cool and the biscuits will harden more in the kitchen.

Store in an airtight container for up to a week.

MINI CAROB AND BANANA MUFFINS

You will be a 'yummy mummy' if you make these for Woofer. Quite a hard texture, not like muffins we would eat but then these are much healthier for your dog!

- ☑ 2 cups of whole wheat flour
- ☑ Half a cup of soybean flour
- ☑ 1 cup of skim milk
- ☑ 1 tablespoon of raw honey
- ☑ 1 tablespoon of sunflower oil
- ☑ Half a cup of carob powder
- ☑ 1 mashed banana
- ☑ 1 tsp of baking powder

Heat oven to 180 C/ 350 F.

Mix together the two flours in a bowl along with the baking powder.

In a separate bowl, mix together the wet ingredients until fully combined.

Add the wet ingredients to the dry, stirring thoroughly until completely combined. The mixture should more or less drop off the spoon, but slightly more dense than a normal cake mixture. If it is too runny, add some more flour.

In a lightly greased muffin tin, spoon the mixture into the individual holes, filling to about three quarters of the way up. Bake in the oven for 25 minutes until very firm to the touch.

Leave to cool. Break into pieces when feeding your dog these lovely muffins.

CHEESY FLAXY HEARTS

Lovely biscuits, make these in two sizes, pocket sized for treats on your training days, and larger ones for 'a good dog, well done' reward.

- ☑ 2 cups of whole wheat flour
- ☑ 2 cups of grated cheddar cheese
- ☑ 1 teaspoon of garlic powder (just this once as a smelly surprise!)
- ☑ Cup of skim milk
- ☑ 1 tablespoon of sunflower oil
- ☑ Half a tablespoon of ground flaxseed

Heat oven to 180 C/350 F. Spray a little (very little) oil spray on to a baking sheet.

Mix together the flour and the cheese. (You could substitute a little of the cheddar for small amount of parmesan – most dogs love the strong flavour of cheese). Add the garlic powder and the oil and mix together well. Add the milk, a little at a time, as you may not need all of it. You are trying to form a stiff dough for rolling.

On a floured surface, knead the dough for a few minutes, then roll out to just under 1 cm/half an inch thick. Cut into heart shapes, using both or either of your cutters.

Cook for 15 – 20 minutes, remove from the oven and allow to cool. The biscuits will harden somewhat but should still be a little soft and crunchy.

Store in a container in the fridge for up to a week to keep fresh. If you think your dog is going to eat them faster than that and you don't have any other treats, leave them in a container out of the fridge.

MORE THAN MEATY MOUTHFULS

Be creative with these dog biscuits and make bone shapes yourself! No cutters on these due to the ingredients!

- ☑ 225 grams/4oz of lean ground beef (uncooked)
- ☑ Quarter of a cup of doggie broth
- ☑ Quarter of a cup of black beans, mashed
- ☑ Third of a cup of low fat cottage cheese
- ☑ 1 teaspoon of soy sauce (special treat!)

Heat the oven to 185 C/375 F.

Mix the ground beef and chicken broth in a mixing bowl. Add the black beans and low fat cottage cheese, then mix in the soy sauce. Make sure all the mixture is thoroughly combined.

Taking some mixture at a time, mould into bone shapes on a lightly floured surface. If you want to experiment, try other shapes!

Place on a baking sheet and bake for about 45 minutes. Leave to cool. The bones should be fairly hard and a good workout for the teeth!

PUMPKIN AND PEANUT BUTTER ICE CREAM

Every dog deserves a bowl of ice cream at his or her party, and this one is very natural and would do no harm to your dog at all. Like everything else, treats should be given in moderation, not just because doggy is putting his paw down and saying, 'I don't fancy that – give me some ice cream!' This recipe makes quite a lot, so make sure you have some plastic tubs to freeze it down.

- ☑ 850 grams/30 oz of natural pure pumpkin puree
- ☑ Half a cup of peanut butter
- ☑ 1 cup of 0% plain yoghurt

Mix all of the ingredients together, stirring well to make sure everything is combined. Place in your plastic tub/s and freeze. After about an hour, take out of the freezer and mix around again. Replace in the freezer for another 2 hours. Take out and stir one more time and leave in the freezer until ready to serve – simple!

Watch out for dirty faces when they dive into this ice cream!

ICY TREATS FOR HOT DOGGIES!

Here are three different easy treats to make for your dogs on a very hot day, or when they have been playing at their party. You need to have some ice cube trays for these treats.

Frozen Banana Treats

Simply peel and cut up a very ripe banana. Lay the slices on to a flat tray and place in the freezer. When they have completely frozen, put into plastic bags and put back in the freezer ready for use – try eating them yourself!

Apple Popsicles

Most dogs love ice cubes, but this is a little more of a treat.

Mix together any low sugar fresh fruit juice, but in this case we have used apple juice, with an equal amount of water. Pour into an ice cube tray and freeze until ready for use, popping one out at a time. Fantastic for a hot day and after a long walk.

Fruit and Freeze Treats

So easy and so tasty for a hot dog! Using an ice cube tray, fill each cube section with berries such as blueberries or strawberries. Add a little water into each cube and freeze, ready for use. Lip-smacking Luxury for cooling down.

BIG BOYS (OR GIRLS!) BIRTHDAY CAKE

Now this one does need some effort. Firstly, as we are quite creative, you need a 'bundt' tin, a cake tin with the hollow bit inside. These are readily available in most hardware stores. If this is all 'a bit too much effort' you can still use the recipe to make a normal cake in a normal cake tin. Make sure you lightly grease the inside of the tin before pouring in the mixture.

We prefer to use minced chicken or turkey due to the high protein and low fat content of the meat.

- ☑ 350 grams/12 oz of minced chicken or turkey
- ☑ 4 eggs
- ☑ Half a cup of oatmeal
- ☑ 1 cup of all-purpose flour
- ☑ 1 tsp of baking powder
- ☑ Half a cup of vegetable oil (or corn oil)
- ☑ Half a cup of carrots, grated
- ☑ You can also add some chopped parsley or mint or even rosemary to add more flavour to this surprise cake

Heat oven to 175 C/350 F.

Using a food processor, put the chicken or turkey mince in with the eggs and the oil and pulse for one minute. Make sure the mixture is combined. If you want a smoother texture, pulse again so that the minced meat is more pulverised.

In a separate bowl, mix the flour and baking powder together, along with the oatmeal, making sure they are all combined together. Add the carrots, and mix again. Make a well in the centre of the dry mix, and gradually pour in the wet mix, stirring thoroughly until completely combined. You can add the herbs at this stage as well.

Pour the mixture into the greased tin, and bake for 45 minutes, until the cake is tender to touch. Test with a skewer to make sure it is cooked all the way through.

Leave to cool in the tin, and when easy to handle, tip out the cake. You may need to loosen the cake round the edges. If using the bundt tin, turn the tin over on to a flat surface, shake gently, tap on the bottom of the tin to ease removal of the cake.

Allow to cool thoroughly before icing (if required). We have decorated the centre of the cake with 'bone biscuits', but please use your imagination and decorate however you want with HEALTHY treats.

DOGGIE FROSTING

You can make dog friendly icing using low fat cream cheese and a little drop of vanilla essence, just this once as a special treat – after all, they only have one birthday a year!

PUPPIES –

HANDLE WITH

CARE!!

OUR PRECIOUS PUPS

Nothing like a newborn puppy to get the 'oohs and aahs' coming out of people. So cute – but they do need to be handled with care. Taken away from mother and her milk, a poor pup can get quite phased, particularly if you don't make the transition of environments as easy on them as possible.

Make your new addition as comfy as possible, he will be missing mum and his playful brothers and sisters. Lots of kisses and cuddles, but that's the easy part – we all love cuddling puppies, but do try not to crowd him/her with too many people at a time and over-excite them. BUT do introduce them to people and situations around your home as soon as you can – the earlier the better to familiarize them with washing machine noises and vacuum cleaners! A nervous puppy can make a nervous dog which can cause defensive reactions that they don't really mean.

Take your breeder's advice – use the food that they should supply you with that the puppy has been eating other than from his mother. Gradually change the puppy's diet – don't do it all in once, their tummies are sensitive and you may not like the results! It's a sound idea to take pup to your vet shortly after acquiring your new addition – they can check that the pup is healthy and recommend any medical treatments immediately, should pup be looking off colour.

It goes without saying that your puppy should have had his first set of jabs before he leaves his original home, and that he should be micro-chipped. Be safe, rather than sorry and check that you have all the necessary certificates proving that this pup has come from a diligent breeder.

Puppies need to be fed little and often – several times a day, as they have tiny stomachs and need constant nutrition until they are about 6 months old, when they can be fed twice a day, just like adults. 3 to 4 times a day when they are very young, with 3 times being around about 4 months old. Pups will devour anything and everything, so beware!

Here are just a couple of simple recipes to gradually introduce to pup's tummy.

PUPPY SLOW COOKED CHOW

This is a great recipe for cooking in your slow cooker, you can just put it all in and forget about it for 6-7 hours.

- ☑ Half cup of carrots, chopped into smallish pieces
- ☑ Half a cup of zucchini/courgettes, chopped into smallish pieces
- ☑ 1 kg/2lbs of boneless, skinless chicken or turkey, cut into small pieces
- ☑ Half a cup of diced apple (ensure skin, all pips and core removed)
- ☑ 1 small can of sardines (not in tomato sauce!)
- ☑ 2 and half cups of brown rice
- ☑ 4 tbsp of olive oil
- ☑ 7 cups of fresh water (boiled is a good idea)

Prepare all the ingredients as above. Place in the slow cooker and leave to cook for between 6-7 hours. Test the rice – if the rice is soft and ready to eat, then the whole dish will be ready.

You can use beef or lamb in this recipe, but it does have a higher fat content.

Makes lots and lots of puppy sized meals! If in doubt about how much to feed your pup in one session, consult your vet. They may also recommend the addition of a puppy vitamin supplement, but this dish includes enough essential nutrients for your little furry friend!

MINI PUP MEATLOAVES

You may need to invest in some tiny meatloaf tins, it really is worth it as portion size is pretty accurate, and you can of course use the tins afterwards for home baking of little loaves or loaf cakes. You need a size of about 14cm (5/half inches) x 8cm (3/half inches) or thereabouts.

- ☑ 450 grams/1lb of lean minced beef
- ☑ 675 grams/24 oz cottage cheese
- ☑ 4 eggs (reserve the shells)
- ☑ Half cup of dry milk powder
- ☑ Half cup of wheatgerm
- ☑ 8 cups of cooked oatmeal, as per packet instructions
- ☑ 4 cups of cooked brown rice, as per packet instructions
- ☑ 6 slices of oatmeal bread, crusts removed and bread crumbled
- ☑ 1 small tin of baby apple sauce or puree (natural)

Heat oven to 175 C/350 F. Lightly grease the baking tins.

Combine beef, cheese together. Add the eggs, milk powder and wheat germ. Then mix in the cooked oatmeal, cooked rice and crumbled bread. Grind 2 or 3 of the eggshells you have reserved into a fine powder if possible (you could use a coffee grinder or spice grinder for this). Add apple sauce and shells to the mixture, and stir everything thoroughly until well mixed together. The mixture should be moist but not runny.

Scoop the mixture into the greased loaf tins and bake for 50 minutes, but test at about 40 minutes to see how it is going. Should be firm to the touch, you can always use a skewer to test, which should come out reasonably clean.

You can freeze these meatloaves for up to 4 weeks in the freezer, or keep a couple of them in the fridge for 4-5 days.

TAKE CARE

OF SENIOR

CITIZENS!

Unique care is required in our latter years, and dogs are certainly no different, and the only way you will know when your dog is approaching his 'senior citizen' era, is by his general slowing down, slight changes in demeanour and less likely to have massive bursts of energy when his lead is shaken to go out for a walk!

Older dogs (somewhere around 8-9 years, but there is no hard and fast rule) need more nutrition, but LESS food. Generally, they will probably doze a bit more, but another sign can be that their joints are a lot stiffer and they don't raise themselves up so easily.

Exercise is still of paramount importance, with a couple of good 20 minutes or so walks a day. They still yearn to be mentally stimulated, so keep up that side of their activity and continue to play games with them that they enjoy.

WATCH YOUR DOGS WEIGHT. This is extremely important, as excess weight puts more pressure on their joints (no different to us!). They won't want to run around as much as they usually do, so calories will not be burnt off at the same rate as younger dogs.

It is also crucial that you do your best to keep joint mobility at the highest possible level. If in any doubt, do visit your vet and ask advice on any ways to help or improve this mobility – they frequently can suggest treatments that do not involved 'chemical' forms of tablets, and can recommend more natural or homeopathic aids to help your dog.

'Oily' fish, such as in our Salmon and Tuna bake, mackerel, sardines etc are definitely beneficial in joint mobility as they are full of Omega 3s, nature's own remedy or help. Comforting dishes such as

Chicken Stew are also good, easy on the stomach with good quality protein, and with the additional of vegetables and fruits, your dogs' immune system will also benefit.

Take care of your 'old soldier' – in his mind, he has been taking care of you for years!

SAVE THE DATE...

HALLOWEEN,

THANKSGIVING OR

CHRISTMAS CHEER

HALLOWEEN HOUND WINTER WARMER

Why not let your dog celebrate Halloween – if you are having a party for yourselves or your children, or a family get together, let him join in as well! When the weather is cold, wet and damp, doggie will appreciate a bit of warmth and tender loving care.

- ☑ 400 grams/14 oz pumpkin, peeled and chopped into small pieces
- ☑ 50 grams/2 oz rice
- ☑ 300 grams/11 oz minced lamb
- ☑ 1 tsp of dried mixed herbs
- ☑ 1 peeled, cored and chopped apple

Preheat oven to 180 C/350 F.

Roast the pumpkin in the oven for 25 minutes in a suitable roasting tin.

Put the rice into a saucepan with boiling water, and simmer until cooked and soft, probably about 10 minutes. Drain and set aside.

Dry fry the lamb for about 10-15 minutes, shaking and stirring to prevent clumps and to ensure the lamb is cooked through. Mix in the apple and continue to heat and stir for a few minutes. Add the herbs and mix thoroughly.

Add the rice and pumpkin to the mince and combine, again making sure everything is mixed thoroughly.

Leave to cool, and then serve to the hungry hounds with watering mouths!

Can be stored in the fridge for up to 4 days.

CHRISTMAS OR THANKSGIVING – DONT LEAVE ME OUT!!

There is no reason why your pet should be left out on these special occasions. Most of what we eat on these two occasions can be shared with them (not scraps off your plate or feeding from the table!) but their very own portion. Turkey is of course very good for dogs with its high protein level, and vegetables speak for themselves. A little treat of sausage is also not a problem, as long as not given on a regular basis.

- ☑ 250 grams/8 oz of cooked turkey from your bird
- ☑ 1 cooked chipolata or small sausage
- ☑ A few cooked carrots
- ☑ 2 tablespoons of cooked peas
- ☑ 100 grams/4 oz of mashed potato, or sweet potato.
- ☑ 50 grams/2 oz of cooked brussel sprouts or cabbage

Chop all the meat ingredients up into small pieces, and mix in with the mashed potatoes or sweet potatoes and brussel sprouts/cabbage. Stir everything together with one tablespoon of your gravy (as long as there is no wine in it!), otherwise leave dry or add a little doggy stock.

POOCHES PUMPKIN CRUMBLE

No reason, with the way this is made, that your dog can enjoy a 'dessert' maybe as an early supper for him. The addition of nutmeg and ginger spices not only add flavour to the pumpkin, but also have health benefits for joints and anti-inflammatory properties.

- ☑ 225 grams/8 oz of peeled and chopped pumpkin
- ☑ Half a teaspoon of nutmeg
- ☑ Sprinkling of ground ginger
- ☑ 50 grams/2 oz of roughly chopped sunflower seeds
- ☑ 50 grams/2 oz of spelt flour or wholemeal flour
- ☑ 50 grams/2 oz of wheat germ
- ☑ 1 tablespoon <u>of</u> blackstrap molasses

Heat the oven to 180 /350 F.

Prepare the 'crumble' topping by mixing the sunflower seeds, wheat germ flour and molasses together. Set aside.

Cook the pumpkin in water until tender. Drain and mix in the ginger and nutmeg. Mash together until thoroughly combined.

Put the pumpkin mixture into a small dish and smooth over the crumble mix. Bake in the oven for approx 10-15 minutes, until slightly chewy and crunchy on the top.

Serve when cool. Any remaining pumpkin crumble can be kept in the fridge for a couple of days.

Hi Mummy –

I don't feel well...

DOGGIES THAT ARE NOT WELL

From time to time, unfortunately, our dogs will be unwell, due to a variety of reasons, mostly something mild that can be dealt with easily. You never know what your dog will pick up on his walk, something he shouldn't eat, or getting too near other dogs faeces, and particularly fox feces, which can cause extreme discomfort to your dog. He may also pick up common dog diseases such as kennel cough or scientifically known as Canine Tracheobronchitis. Whilst some dog owners will treat kennel cough themselves, it is advisable for you to take your dog to your vet, to cure it faster and relieve your dog as soon as possible. Kennel Cough causes great discomfort to your dog, and a high level of distress, so do not wait until you think you can sort it out yourself.

In terms of upset tummies, probably the most regular occurrence with dogs, always keep an eye on your dogs' POOPS and also his urine colour etc. You should do this as a matter of course all the time, as it is a clear indication as to how your dog is, and whether he or she is digesting food properly. Generally, POOP should be light brown to medium brown in colour, and of a firm consistency, so that when you pick it up, very little is left on the grass or ground.

So back to the reasons for making your home made dog food. Good quality wet food or homemade food is more easily and properly digested, due to the whole ingredients with which it is made, so what actually comes out is waste and fibre, rather than a lot of indigestible 'rubbish'.

Poor quality dog food contains a lot of commercial ingredients that fail to get broken down via your dogs' digestive system, resulting in LOTS MORE POOP!! A lot of people who have changed to making their own dog food remark on the reduction in the amount of excretions, and also that, in fact, it doesn't smell so pungent. Well whoopee to that one!

Just be vigilant regarding your dog in terms of his or her stools. Watch the colour, and if the stools are very, very dark or black, they may have eaten too much meat, so re-balance the diet with some vegetables and some carbohydrates.

The most important thing to remember – ALWAYS CONSULT YOUR VET IF SYMPTOMS PERSIST for more than a couple of days. They really are the best source of diagnosis, you will have done your part by monitoring any changes in normal stomach behaviour.

If your dog does have a tummy infection, your vet will sometimes recommend a course of antibiotics, and some simple food, such as poached fish or poached chicken with perhaps some plain rice. Normally your dog's stomach will return to normal very rapidly.

Other good soothing meals for dogs who may for instance have had a bout of diarrhoea, can be made up of a little pasta, or some oats or even mashed carrot and potato.

A couple of simple recipes would be:

PLAIN TURKEY PASTA BROTH

- ☑ 100 grams/4 oz dried pasta
- ☑ A small palm full of finely shredded cooked turkey
- ☑ 1 low salt chicken or turkey stock cube

Cook the pasta according to packet instructions, but add a low salt stock cube to the water.

Drain off the pasta, but reserve just a little of the liquid. Put the chicken into the saucepan, and mix with the pasta. Leave to cool, and only serve a little amount to start with, keep it easy on the tummy.

PLAIN OAT MIXTURE

If your dog has been unwell, try to remember to cook off some oats last thing at night, or first thing in the morning, so they have time to cool down. They are very soothing and also provide some energy and strength to a doggie that may have been a little wiped out after an upset tummy. Simply boil 100 grams/4 oz of oats with 600ml/1 pint of water for about ten minutes, then leave to cool.

RAW FOOD –

TO SERVE OR

NOT TO SERVE?

RAW FOOD DIET

This is a controversial subject to say the least, and in this book we would not be prepared to say 'yay or nay' on the subject. Popularity of the raw food diet for dogs has risen dramatically since 1993, and is advocated by Australian Vet, Ian Billinghurst, who first brought it to the attention of dog owners after many years of research. Now commonly called the 'BARF' diet (Bones And Raw Food) or Biologically Appropriate Raw Food, it has been the subject of controversy in the veterinarian world for several years.

So what is BARF? We all know that domestic dogs descended from wolves and other wild dogs, who foraged in the wild and whose only source of nourishment was any meat or road kill style of food they could scavenge, topped up with wild vegetables and berries etc., but primarily raw meat.

But dogs stomachs have changed over the years due to domesticity and over a period of time have adopted a more modified and readily available diet that owners rightly or wrongly, are prepared to provide. But all diets, whether human or dog, come with benefits and pitfalls and owners should be aware of this.

Benefits of BARF

Supporters of the BARF diet, both qualified and unqualified, promote the following:

☑ Shinier Coats
☑ Healthier Skin
☑ Cleaner Teeth and breath
☑ Higher Energy Levels

Smaller 'poops' !

Pitfalls of BARF

There are obviously pitfalls, which the advocates of BARF do concur with.

- ☑ Bacterial exposure to HUMANS and dogs from raw meat
- ☑ Unbalanced diet over an extended period of time
- ☑ Raw whole bones – choking potential, breaking of teeth, internal lodging of bones resulting in puncture of organs.

Wholesale dog food manufacturers have somewhat jumped on the bandwagon and now produce commercially processed raw food that is either frozen or freeze-dried. Some of the manufacturers produce raw meat mixes that contain grains and vegetables, with added vitamins.

Raw food diets should comprise of a mixture of raw meat, vegetables (green and leafy are preferable), some fruits such as apples or berries, bones (whole or ground), raw eggs, some dairy such as yoghurt and the addition of some organ meat, such as liver or kidney.

There are pros and cons for any diet that you feed your dogs, no different to human food. Getting the right balance can be tricky.

The best situation is always to test your dog, once you have determined that your dog is healthy and has no underlying illnesses. ALWAYS as we have emphasised, consult your vet and ask for their advice, and certainly a health check on your pet before embarking on any radical changes to the food that you provide. The fact that so many veterinarians have different opinions, is indicative of the indecision as to what is better and what could potentially be detrimental to your pet. The decision is yours at the end of the day.

HOW TO PREPARE A RAW FOOD DIET FOR DOGS

The most important thing is to weigh your dog to ascertain how much raw food to feed each day.

Dr Billinghurst advises feeding amounts of between 2 and 3 per cent of your dog's body weight i.e.

Half a pound of food per 25lb (11.3kg) in weight

Puppies should not be fed more than 10 per cent of their body weight. Lazy dogs should be fed the minimum of the recommended daily intake.

Most people using the raw food diet for their dogs use these measurements as a guideline

- ☑ Approx 80% muscle meat with fat
- ☑ Approx 10% organ meat
- ☑ Approx 10% raw meaty bones
- ☑ Eggs – once a week, preferably raw
- ☑ Green Tripe – can make up 15-18% of overall diet

Green tripe is considered to be the most nutritious part of a raw diet and important to include.

Always use the freshest meats and organs available, preferably organic if you can find and afford it.

Mix with low glycemic vegetables, if you choose so, such as spinach and carrots.

USEFUL

EQUIPMENT FOR

DOGGIE

COOKING!

USEFUL EQUIPMENT FOR DOGGIE COOKING!

As you probably realize, most of the equipment in your household kitchen is more than enough to cope with cooking meals for your dog. However, it would always be useful to get extra utensils and cooking pots and trays. Equally so, make sure you have plenty of airtight containers and freezer bags, as well as just normal plastic tear-off food bags, useful for your pockets when on a dog walk.

IF YOU ARE REALLY SERIOUS ABOUT MAKING YOUR OWN DOG FOOD, here is a recommendation that we do advocate.

DEHYDRATOR

This is a really good purchase if you want to make your own dried dog food, such as liver treats or other chewy treats for your dog. There are a multitude of dehydrators on the market from small to large and almost industrial size.

Smaller dehydrators do work, although you can only prepare a certain amount of food at a time. These usually vary in price – you can pick up a dehydrator online through the normal channels such as Amazon or Ebay. They would cost anywhere from $30 - $100 USD (£20-£60) depending on the facilities they have – no different to buying any other piece of kitchen food equipment.

However, as we say, if you are serious about making your own dog treats etc., do invest in a larger more sophisticated one – you can make a weeks' worth of treats in one go. These do normally cost around $250 USD (£160) but they do warrant the extra expenditure, if, and only if, you are dedicated to making the food. Over a period of time you will recoup your outlay, and also be comforted by the fact that what you cook is what your dog gets to eat – no additives, no rubbish! And eventually, it is cheaper!

The one thing for sure is to buy QUALITY MEAT even if it is offal or otherwise. Tried and tested top class butchers will be more than happy to supply you with the cuts of meat that they may not sell so easily.

ALWAYS keep the dehydrator and trays in tip top cleanliness condition, to avoid any bacteria collecting.

If you have space, use a large dehydrator in your garage or outhouse, or other room away from the main kitchen. Apart from health and safety, large quantities of drying food can give off an aroma that clings around the house and gets into your nasal passages!

RECIPES USING A DEHYDRATOR

These recipes are ideal for a dehydrator, but can also be cooked in the oven – the drawback of using the oven is the length of time it will take to dry out the food items enough to make them either chewy or crunchy! Whichever way, you avoid nasty artificial ingredients and make healthy treats for your four-legged friend.

CHICKEN OR BEEF JERKY STRIPS

A perfect snack for your dog, all natural ingredients and easy to make.

- ☑ 1lb/450 grams of lean beef or boneless, skinless chicken breasts, trimmed of any fat.
- ☑ Half a cup of vegetable oil
- ☑ Seasonings such as rosemary, parsley or sage

Set the dehydrator to 140 C/280 F.

Cut the chicken or beef into really thin strips, about half a centimetre or ¼ inch thick. Remember to slice along the 'grain' of the meat, not against it.

Put into a bowl with the oil and any seasonings you have chosen. Toss the chicken with the oil and seasonings so the strips are completely coated.

Place the meat strips across the entire tray, leaving a gap between each strip to enable the air to flow between them and the drying out process can be done properly. Cook for approx 3 hours, then test to see if the meat is of the required dryness. If not, continue for a further hour. You can leave it longer if you want, but test a strip after three hours – it should be cooked and the same colour all the way through. The longer you leave the strips, the drier and more chewy they become.

Once cool, store in airtight containers or in freezer bags, in or out of the fridge depending how long you want to preserve them.

Do experiment with your dehydrator with fruits and vegetables, the end result is quite satisfying. Try to use herbs and spices (nutmeg, cinnamon etc) to make the dishes really tasty for your dog.

SUNFLOWER SHAPES

Just like a crunchy dog biscuit, full of vitamins and a slightly sweeter tasting biscuit for your dog.

- ☑ ¼ cup of sunflower seeds
- ☑ 2 cups of spelt or wholemeal flour
- ☑ ½ cup of chopped apples
- ☑ ¼ cup of carrots, peas or other vegetable, finely chopped
- ☑ ¼ cup of powdered oats (not sweet)
- ☑ 1 cup of peanut butter
- ☑ 1 cup of blackstrap molasses
- ☑ 1 cup of normal rolled oats

Set the dehydrator to 150 C/300 F.

Mix all the ingredients together, excluding the molasses. Add the molasses once the ingredients are thoroughly combined. Work the mix into a stiff dough.

Roll the dough out to desired thickness. Cut into any shape you require using your cutters.

Dehydrate for approx 4-5 hours, checking after 4 hours is up. Biscuits should be very dry.

THE

IMPORTANCE OF

YOUR VET...

One of the most important people in your life and your dogs' life is your VETERINARIAN.

When you first acquire your pet, if you have never done so before, PLEASE register him or her with your local vet and try to organise an appointment for a health check immediately you take your doggie home. Certainly with puppies, they may not be as healthy as you thought, even though when you pick them up for the first time, you are greeted with licks and wagging tails. They could be suffering from various minor illnesses, particularly if they have been purchased from an unregistered breeder or puppy farm.

You should get a 'feel' of your puppy's upbringing when you visit the breeder for the first time. Check the conditions they have been living in – is it clean, do the puppies look happy and healthy, are their eyes and ears clear, and when walking or running, are they steady and not limping? Any sores or wounds?

Primarily, the puppie's mother should be in residence with her pups and preferably the father too, but this is not always possible. These simple checks can alleviate any heartache of having to return the puppy to the breeder if there is an underlying illness or condition that may have been hidden from you.

Also make sure that you receive an authorised breeding certificate or registration with the appropriate governing body, as this will tell you the breeding history of your dog. You should also receive a 'health check' form from the breeder's vet – showing tests of all the obvious faculties of your new pet – eyes, ears and also 'hip scores'. Certain breeds are susceptible to joint problems at birth, so wise to check this out before taking your puppy home.

MICROCHIPPING

Microchipping gives you peace of mind, but more importantly it gives your pet the best chance of being identified and reunited with you, if lost or stolen.

Many dogs go missing, it is their natural instinct to roam free, but theft of dogs is on the increase every year, particularly popular pedigree breeds, as they change hands for a considerable 'booty' for the uncaring thieves that steal beloved pets.

Microchipping is becoming compulsory in many countries in the next few years. A tiny microchip is inserted under the dog's skin, which gives you a unique 'ID' code. Scanning the chip provides details of owners and contact details which are kept on a central database. In theory, most pets are microchipped by the breeder before they go home with you, but if not, make sure you visit your vet and get this quick and painless service done for your dog. It only take a few seconds, rather than months of pain and upset to you when your home is empty of your canine family member.

Microchipping is only effective if you keep your details up to date. If you move house or change your telephone number, make sure that you update the central database with these significant alterations.

DIAGNOSIS

It cannot be reiterated enough that when in doubt, take your dog to your vet for diagnosis of any ailments or allergies that may be affecting his or her wellbeing.

Vets have not spent many years training for no reason. Life threatening complaints such as heart disease or diabetes will be easily diagnosed by your vet with a series of tests, all of which are painless to your pet.

Likewise any form of allergies can be diagnosed by this learned professional. Once diagnosed, diet will play an important part in the continuing health of your dog.

It is wise not to embark on any form of diet for your dog unless you have consulted with your vet.

DOGS WITH HEART PROBLEMS

Your vet, and only your vet can diagnose whether your dog has heart problems and whether they are mild, medium or chronic. They will also be able to recommend a suitable diet for your dog to include the necessary vitamins and minerals to combat the problem. Dogs would usually develop diabetes around the age of 7 or 8, but just in humans, it can develop earlier or later.

Vets will probably recommend home prepared dishes for your dog, using whole natural foods which create health and vitality, whereas processed dog foods can foster and create disease. Some will also advocate raw food diets.

Most pet foods on the market contain ingredients that are unable to make it into the human food chain, thereby ending up in pet food. It may look and smell wholesome, but can be full of 'unnatural' ingredients. However, your vet will no doubt recommend certain elements of a commercially produced dog food, normally a scientific diet, to supplement what you are making. They will also recommend supplements including oils and naturally produced additions to the diet, that possibly your dog will need.

The recipe below is a very basic wholesome combination, but PLEASE check this out with your vet before commencing any form of changes in diet.

Simple Chicken and Rice Meal

This recipe will feed a dog weighing around 12-13 kgs/30 lbs. You can adjust the quantities to suit the weight of your dog. You should get two days' worth of servings out of these amounts.

- ☑ 3 and a half cups of cooked boneless, skinless chicken breast, diced
- ☑ 2 and a half cups of cooked brown rice, long grain
- ☑ 2 cups of pureed fruit or vegetables
- ☑ 2 tbsp of organic plant based oil (contains 3,6 and 9 omegas. Check with your vet.)

DOGS WITH DIABETES

There are varying degrees of diabetes, just as in humans. You cannot possibly diagnose diabetes yourself, but if your dog is excessively thirsty, and a bit debilitated, please take them to the vet, where a simple blood test with check out whether they have a diabetic problem. Listen to your vet, they know best and can prescribe correct medication to alleviate the problem.

The following recipe is a wholesome recipe that contains nutrients to assist in the control of diabetes, but by no means recommended until after you consult your vet.

Chicken, Rice and Vegetable Combo (can be made with very lean beef also)

- ☑ 1 cup of cooked brown rice, long grain
- ☑ 1 cup of cooked skinless, boneless chicken breast, or very lean beef.
- ☑ Half cup of cooked green beans, cabbage or broccoli
- ☑ Half cup of other cooked vegetables, such as carrots and peas
- ☑ Half cup of cottage cheese, low fat

This recipe will feed a dog of 12-13kg/30 lbs, for two meals. It is not recommended for freezing.

ALWAYS CONSULT YOUR VET. They will recommend other nutritional supplements that will complete the programme to help your dog.

We do not advocate any treatment by way of these recipes and strongly recommend that you take your vet's advice at all times.

DOGS WITH

ALLERGIES

There are a multitude of dog allergies, but generally they can be broken down into three categories:

- Flea allergy dermatitis
- Food allergies
- Environmental allergies

It is obviously extremely important to relieve your suffering hound of any allergic reactions caused by the above, and again, if your dog is suffering, please consult your vet who will be able to ascertain which allergy your dog has, and how to treat it from the inside and out. Your vet should work with you to isolate what is the cause of the problem, and will not necessarily recommend a course of anti-allergy or antibiotic drugs or anti-viral medications. If the problem is dietary based, then results can be achieved by treating the problem at source, with special selected diets.

FAD (FLEA ALLERGY DERMATITIS)

Caused by the saliva of a flea, not the actual bite, this is a common cause of itching and scratching in dogs. You may be convinced that your dog does not have fleas, but the saliva is the root cause and can make your dog miserable and uncomfortable.

Grooming plays a big part in the care of your dog, and during the pest season, it is best to comb your dog twice a day with a flea comb. If you do this on a light surface, you will see what is coming off your dog. Likewise bathing – a soothing bath removes most fleas and makes dogs less 'attractive' to infestation, and also assists in stopping your dog from scratching.

Do make use of natural pest repellents for fleas and ticks, as they do provide a defence against these nasty individuals that can cause your dog so much discomfort.

FOOD ALLERGIES AND REACTIONS

An allergy to a particular kind of food can manifest itself in many ways, not just an upset stomach.

- Itchy and broken skin
- Itchy and irritated red eyes
- Red and inflamed ears
- Breathing problems, coupled with coughing or excess sneezing
- Discharge from the nose

There are various saliva tests that can be made to ascertain what allergy your dog is suffering from, but some vets will use an 'elimination' diet to get to the source of the problem. Over a period of time, certain foods will be taken out, and then put back in to your dog diet as a slow process.

One of the most common food allergies for dogs is gluten, but there are obviously many more.

ENVIRONMENTAL ALLERGIES

A lot more difficult to diagnose, as your pet could be allergic to many things in the home or the outside environment. There are a few tips to assist in finding out what irritates your dog.

- Use non-toxic cleaning products indoors
- Try to control dust mites, an air purifier can help in this
- Keep your dog well-bathed at all times
- Fresh drinking water with low fluoride

Try to clean your dog's paws after every walk —outside allergies often begin by getting in to your dog's feet. This will also stop them from 'tramping' it through the house and re-contracting.

GLUTEN FREE RECIPES

Gluten is a common cause of allergies in dogs. We cannot possibly suggest recipes for every allergy, but here are a couple of recipes to counteract reactions to gluten.

Gluten Free Meatballs

- ☑ 450 grams/1lb of lean minced beef or pork
- ☑ 2 large carrots
- ☑ 2 tablespoons of hard cheese
- ☑ 2 tablespoons of gluten free brown breadcrumbs
- ☑ 2 tbsp of peas
- ☑ 1 large egg
- ☑ 1 tbsp of apple puree or baby food

Heat oven to 175C/350F.

Using a food processor, put the carrots and the cheese in and chop finely, not quite to a mush, leaving some texture.

Put the meat and breadcrumbs into a bowl and combine thoroughly. Add the carrot and cheese mixture, followed by the peas, and mix again. Add the apple puree/baby food and stir in until everything is combined.

Form into small balls and bake for 15-20 minutes. Leave to cool and then serve.

Chicken/Lambs Liver Pasta

- ☑ 110 grams/4oz lambs liver/chicken livers cut into small pieces
- ☑ 110 grams/4oz of cooked gluten free pasta
- ☑ 110 grams/4oz of cooked peas
- ☑ A little water
- ☑ Half a tablespoon of olive oil
- ☑ 1 level tablespoon of chopped parsley

Sauté the liver in a small amount of olive oil until cooked. Drain off any excess oil.

Mix the cooked pasta, peas and parsley together with the chicken livers/lambs liver. Add a little water to moisten. Serve when cool enough for doggie to eat.

WHEAT ALLERGY

Some dogs suffer from a wheat and gluten allergy, so here is a delicious recipe to alleviate both of those allergies.

Carrot and Cinnamon Buttons

- ☑ 2 cups of rice flour
- ☑ 2 teaspoons of cinnamon
- ☑ 2 cups of gluten free oats
- ☑ 1 cup of carrot, finely grated
- ☑ 2 tbsp of blackstrap molasses
- ☑ 2 eggs, beaten
- ☑ A little water for moisture
- ☑ 1 cup of baby apple food, or sugar free apple puree/sauce

Heat oven to 175C/350F. Cover two baking trays with parchment paper.

Mix the rice, oats and cinnamon together in a bowl. In a separate bowl, mix together the carrots, apple, eggs and molasses. Add a little water to make mixing easier.

Make a well in the centre of the dry mix, and pour in the wet mix. Combine thoroughly. The mixture should be semi-moist, if not, add a little more water.

'Drop' the mixture on to the baking trays in small amounts, about half a tablespoon size, keeping them apart.

Bake for approx 20 minutes – the buttons should be golden brown. Remove from the oven and leave to cool enough to handle. Place the buttons on a wire rack to cool completely before serving to your dog. You may like to try one yourself, they are pretty delicious!

A SHINY COAT

PLEASE!!...

DOG GROOMING

Taking care of your dog on the outside is equally as important as keeping his insides healthy with a well-balanced diet. What your dog eats will affect his external appearance, both skin and coat.

Regular grooming is of the essence, to remove dead hair and to check out any infestation. Make sure you have adequate tools for the job, particularly if you have a big and hairy beast! The tools that you use will of course depend on your breed of dog.

Useful tools include:

- Brushes and combs
- Clipper or trimmer
- De-matting comb or brush
- Grooming mitt
- Dog scissors (these can be purchased with a protective 'bull nose' to prevent cutting your dog)
- Shedding blades and rakes (useful for very hairy dogs, such as Old English Sheepdogs, Border Collies, etc)

- Any matting that occurs on your dog can actually cause them a considerable amount of pain, so getting rid of old hair on a very regular basis is of prime importance. Oils in your dog's diet will always aid in providing a healthy, glossy coat, but as he/she cannot comb their own hair, it is important that you look after their skin and coat health, let alone making sure they look their best at all times!

- Try to groom your dog at least once a day, using appropriate tools, and where possible, particularly if they are adventurous dogs on their walks, add another combing or grooming sessions. Try to de-matt regularly, to prevent a build-up of unwanted and irritating old hair.

- We have not mentioned nail clippers – a lot of owners really find this a blood curdling experience. Better to leave this to a professional groomer if you are even slightly worried.

Clipping a dog's nails or claws to short can cause them pain and bleeding.

DOG BATHING

Another very important item as a dog owner. NEVER use human shampoo, most of them contain ingredients that are not beneficial to your dogs' skin and coat, and can cause irritation. There are many dog shampoos on the market, but in fact you can make a great shampoo yourself with natural and non-irritant ingredients. Always make sure that the water is of ambient temperature, so that you do not scald your dog or that they can get too cold, especially small dogs who suffer from extremes of cold. Try to accustom your dog to bathing at an early age; it makes life a lot easier!

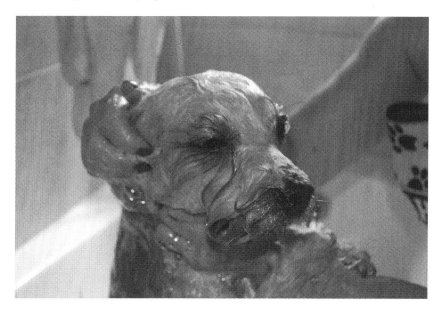

Plenty of CLEAN dog towels are also essential. If you do not use clean towels for every bath, there may be infestation residue from the last bath.

Do not worry if your dog looks miserable when being bathed – they are probably quite enjoying the experience, but they just don't want to let you know that!

Lay out everything you need before you start, be prepared – you cannot go wandering off if you forgot something and leave doggie in the bath. Brushes, combs, towels, shampoo and conditioner (if used) cotton balls (for ears), anything you may think you will use.

Put a non-slip mat in the bottom of the bath – pup will then not be skidding around all over the place!

Brush before to remove unnecessary and unwanted hair. Wet from the head down, careful not to get water in your dogs' eyes or ears. Lather gently, and work the shampoo into the coat and skin, as you would your scalp. Keep talking as you would normally to your dog, for reassurance (the dog, not you!)

Rinse off thoroughly, getting all traces of shampoo out of the coat and skin. If you are using conditioner, massage gently into the hair, leave for a minute or so, and then remove, rinsing thoroughly. Towel dry reasonably vigorously to remove as much water as you can. Doggie will love to have a good shake then!

If you can afford a dog dryer, they really do help, but you can use a domestic hairdryer, but ensure that this is on low temperature and low speed, and kept away from the dog as drying him or her, from a distance, rocking the dryer backwards and forwards. Comb your dog as you are drying – this way your find any matted areas that you may have missed.

How to Make a Natural Shampoo

Human shampoo has a lower pH and is too acidic for your dog. Making your own shampoos and conditioner is a very easy and relatively inexpensive process.

- ☑ 3 tbsp of unscented washing liquid (for plates etc) or grate castile soap
- ☑ 4 cups of hot water
- ☑ 1 cup of apple cider vinegar
- ☑ 2 drops of essential oils, such as lavender or chamomile

Put into a squeezable plastic bottle and shake vigorously before use every time. Store in a cool dark place between uses.

How to Make a Natural Conditioner

You may need to experiment a little with this, depending on the size of your dog. Perhaps you may have to lessen the baby oil, as you want a glossy dog, not a greasy one!

- ☑ 1 tbsp of baby oil
- ☑ 1 egg yolk
- ☑ 2 tbsp of water
- ☑ 1 drop of essential oils (rosemary, vanilla, chamomile etc.)

Mix all the ingredients to a frothy consistency. Massage into your dog's coat. Leave for a minute or two, and then wash off thoroughly, the coat should be glossy but not greasy to the touch – and they smell really good too!

INDEX